About the Author

Lauren Hanna is a Happiness Ambassador and Kindness Cultivator. She recently earned a Master's Degree in Clinical Psychology, specializing in the treatment of addiction disorders. Lauren's calling is deeply rooted in restoring love, hope, and dignity to the hearts of homeless individuals. Through her homeless outreach organization, Lunchtime Love, and volunteer work, she aspires to encourage a greater empathy for individuals in need, their unique stories, and every soul's innate worthiness of unconditional love. As a "loving-kindness" blogger, Lauren endeavors to inspire others to live life through a lens of infinite love, kindness, and peace. Lauren currently lives in Chicago, seeking every opportunity to sparkle kindness along the paths of everyone she greets.

For daily love and kindness inspiration, visit Lauren's social media pages:

Blog
LaurenLoveandKindness.Tumblr.com

Instagram
Lauren_LoveandKindness

Twitter
LaurenLoveJoy22

To share your comments/questions about *Prayers Get Answered* or inquire about speaking engagement opportunities, contact Lauren at:

PrayersGetAnsweredBook@gmail.com

Acknowledgments

To God, for His ever-present, loving inspiration in writing this chapter of my soul's journey.

To Joan, Wafik, and Mark, for their unconditional love and encouragement.

To Lisa Cleveland, for opening my heart to the wisdom that love will always overpower fear.

To any soul who is homeless, for demonstrating how compassion, radiant resilience, fervent faith, and joy can transcend all suffering.

Finally, I dedicate this book to every sweet spirit who yearns to experience unconditional love. I pray that each word makes your heart feel heard.

Table of Contents

Introduction	4
Faith, Hope, and Trust	6
Love, Kindness, and Joy	22
Gratitude and Mindfulness	40
The Power of Prayer	49
Forgiveness and Healing	54
Authenticity	61
Dreams	65
Wisdom, Patience, and Understanding	66
Humility	71
Angels and Miracles	73

Introduction

What is it about prayer that is so powerful?

For starters, prayer comes in any style. Whether casual or formal in nature, it does not matter – as long as it suits your *you*-nique journey. Prayer can assume the form of laughter as you gaze up at a lavender and salmon-pink sunset, amazed at how God recently intervened in your life, bestowing His grace at just the right moment. Prayer may also be a deluge of tears, pouring down your face as your heart endeavors to make sense of heartache and tragedy. At times, prayer can be a deep belly sigh signifying a need for more patience and trust in God's grander design. And, on some days, prayer may function as an enthusiastic expression of gratitude for God's glorious gifts; it is the exclamation point at the end of a beautifully blessed day!

Whether the aim honors an individual matter or serves to help a stranger in need, there is no doubt that prayer provides profuse peace. As Oprah Winfrey underscores time and again, at the end of the day, all human beings just want to be heard. Thus, the power of prayer: as a direct, open communication line to God, prayer allows our voices to resound on an unparalleled plane. Prayer echoes our souls' deepest desires and needs. It is a constant chord connecting us with an all-loving presence. What an immense comfort it is to know that we can call upon such an empowering Source of goodness, any time, any place!

Further, the more we align our prayers with God's will, the more God opens our hearts to discern His answers. As I have learned over the past several months, in particular, the stream of silence lingering after certain prayers is often God's loudest answer that He is working for our greater good. However the answers arise, there is one thing I know for sure: God hears each and every single prayer! The myriad miracles I have witnessed over the course of my life continue to punctuate the power of prayer. God is *always* listening with unconditional love.

Certainly, the evolution of this book is its own prayer answered. I had no intention of writing a book, much less a series of prayers in poetry form. Then again, God never ceases to amaze! This year entailed a string of life-changing decisions and self-discoveries. Before I knew it, prayer assumed a more frequent and pivotal role in navigating my daily experiences. During the early morning hours of October 2, 2015, I ambled to the bathroom to brush my teeth and prepare for the day's activities. Without any conscious thought, I prayed aloud, "Lord, may my life be a prayer." As soon as the words crossed my lips, I knew something instantly shifted. There was something peculiar about this prayer request; I experienced a simultaneous sense of awe and joy of which the most blissful adjectives in the English language could not come *close* to capturing. Initially confused, I proceeded to pray aloud. In addition to my daily prayers, I asked God for wisdom to understand the significance of this awe-inspiring prayer. Within an hour, I had effortlessly (i.e., miraculously) composed pages of prayers. My astonishment only elevated as I recognized their rhythmic pattern. Given the rapid rate at which these heart-poems manifested over the next few days, I soon understood one of God's purposes underlying my initial prayer: *Prayers Get Answered*.

My prayer is that this book opens your hearts to the power of prayer, on both an individual and collective level. Whether it centers on fortifying faith and forgiveness, traversing trials with trust, cultivating a mindfulness of God's multiple miracles, or inspiring acts of love and kindness, I pray that each prayer instills a newfound comfort and peace in your sweet soul. I hope that the rhythmic beat and practical application helps you view prayer through a new lens – namely one that transcends a means to an end. Lastly, I pray that this book unveils the sheer joy that is inherent in the prayer *process*.

While we may never meet, please know that I am already praying for you. Please know that you are loved *unconditionally*, and that your purpose in this world is profound simply because you exist! Thank you for being you.

In every prayer, remember that God is always there.

Faith, Hope, and Trust

Understanding God's Divine Time Zone

Lord, help hush our hurried hearts!
Quiet our spirits so that we can hear the wonderfully warm whisper of *Your* time table.
For *this* blindness of trust is what makes us most able!
Open our hearts to the incomparable peace in "the pause."
For when we incessantly seek to impose our own timing,
It is likely You are looking down and simply smiling!

Let us remember that, to You,
The earthly day is like a thousand years.
And, it is in learning to celebrate that telling truth
That we can start to quell our myriad fears!

As You said, man plans but God decides.
It is in our fruitful acceptance of these words
Where peace and Your ultimate will for us resides!

Wisdom of Faith

Lord, may You unveil the wisdom of building blind faith!
The experience of faith is far grander
Than the most perceptive part of the human mind.
But, of course it is!
For faith flows from You!
And *You* are of the Heavenly kind!

Lord, may we understand that faith is *to simply know*.
It is in this space where our trust can truly grow!
It is in this space where faith transcends what we can see or touch.
For faith is a practice of both the happiest *and* heaviest of hearts.
It is a goal,
Born in the sweetest, most sincere spot of the soul!

Inspire

Holy Spirit, inspire!
God, the father,
It is Your glorious gift of fervent faith
For which we always aspire!
Jesus, in Your everlasting example of loving-kindness,
Our spirits shall never tire!

Brave Wave

Lord, shower us with a sea of strength.
Teach us how each turquoise wave
Is an illustration in how to be bold and brave!

Lift our fears.
Wipe away the tears.

Encourage us to rise
By bestowing upon our hearts all that is spiritually wise!

Remind us with every warm whisper of a serene stream,
Our problems are here for You to take.
Our spirits are here for You to gleam.

Bed of Hope
Dedicated to homeless hearts throughout the world

Lord, may You hear the weary whisper of every struggling soul.
May Your endless compassion cover like a beautiful blanket,
Making every lonely heart feel happy and whole!

Radiate waves of warmth and tenderness within their sparkly spirits.
May the most worn and worthy hearts find rest in the fact
That Your ever-present mercy is a pillow of faith.
Despite every tired tear and hovering fear,
Remind them that You are always near!

Chase away every chill
By realigning their hearts with Your miraculous will.

May Your soothing love lap waves of hope
Wonderfully washing away any fear or doubt.
Show their hearts that You will peacefully provide a way out.

Lord, with *You* all things are possible!

For every heart in need who incessantly hears the word "nope,"
Our prayer is that they see Your unconditional love and blessings
As the ultimate bed of hope!

Courage Propels Hope

Lord, teach us what it means to harbor heart-*full* hope,
As sometimes it can feel like an endless game of tug of rope.

Valor is one of the sturdiest spiritual roots grounding everlasting hope.
May You curate *colossal* courage deep down within our souls.
For in doing so, You will fashion a crystal clear route
To crush all self-doubt!

God Is the Best Life Vest

Lord, when we stumble upon storms of self-doubt,
Or we find ourselves sinking in sorrow,
May we knock on Your door for a bit of faith to borrow!

Cast Your loving net of grace and mercy in our direction,
As it elevates us out of darkness' depths
And provides the most peaceful protection!

Remind our hearts that You will never let us drown in despair,
For Your all-encompassing love
Is a constantly cascading fountain of care!

Calm

Lord, when the forecast seems to be clouded with endless burdens,
Drizzle down a blanket of calm.
May we offer up all that we suffer to help heal hearts in need,
All the while casting our cares into Your Heavenly palm.
Inspire us to secure solace in a hope-*full* psalm.
For this can often serve as a soothing spiritual balm!

Every Day Is a Journey

Lord, as we wake this morning,
Bloom in our beings an attitude of gratitude and terrific trust!
For when trying circumstances seem to lurk ahead of us,
These are an absolute must.

When we seek to diligently depend on You, alone,
Our souls cannot help but be restored to their whole.

While these graces are essential to fusing our spirits with Your will,
They will also help us surmount any looming hill.

When we encounter stress
We are confident Your loving-kindness will caress.

Help us take it
One day,
One hour,
One minute,
At a time.

Steer our spirits to remember that a journey of joy
Is to be unearthed in each day.
For this wisdom and understanding, we pray!

Help

Lord...
HELP!
Our request may be super succinct,
But such an exclamation is sometimes the most effective
Prayer-*full* kind of yelp!

Compassionate Compass

Lord, infuse us with Your wonderful wisdom!
May we consider You to be our all-knowing compass and true north.
For when we heed Your divine direction,
Oodles of love and compassion are sent forth!

May You serve as our navigator and peaceful post,
As You are the foremost Heavenly host.

And if we ever lose our way,
May we remember that all we have to do is pray!

Faith Over Fear

Lord, some mornings we wake with heaviness of heart,
Yet with a simple bellow of Your name,
That weary weight can part.

May Your peace purge any trace of fear, anger, and sadness.
And in its stead,
Pour down merriment and gladness.

Before we know it, our minds incessantly ruminate
And question all that is the future.
Remind us to entrust our faith in Your plans,
For then our hearts will be at rest.
Then our spirits can be joyously sure!

You Will Make a Way

Lord, may our hearts spill over with abundant faith and self-belief,
For on many days this will confer the utmost relief!

What a glorious and generous gift it is to remember
That Your luminous light resides in all beings.
To recall that Your Divinity dances within all of us
Remains one of the most revitalizing feelings!

You are all-seeing.
You are always behind us.
All we have to do is *trust*!

Saturate our spirits with blind faith;
The type of assurance that knows You will always make a way.
Oh Lord, You moved mountains!
With five loaves and two fish You fed thousands!
You created the course of each day!
When it comes to Your greatness,
May we remember that anything our hearts can conceive,
With Your grace, Divine will, and timing,
We will receive!

Bold Faith

Lord, we cannot offer enough gratitude for Your presence alongside us every day.
Regardless of the stressors we may encounter,
You always provide a wonderful way.
Whether or not our earthly pencils have sketched into the calendar myriad to-do's,
Remind us to turn to You in all that we choose.

In decisions big and small,
Sometimes our minds and hearts can feel quite harried.
Lord, especially in these moments,
May a simple prayer for strength and wisdom help us feel weightless,
Even carried!

However the day's designs unfold,
Foster our spirits with a faith that is blessed and oh-so bold!

May we look back upon the day's events and wonder,
"How did I do it?"
Then may we recall,
You were right there beside us through it all.
Your loving comfort hugged us the *entire* time!
You filled us with faith to sometimes walk,
And to sometimes climb!

Leaning on Trust

Lord, teach us how to totally trust!
Help us to seek solace in all that is Divinely just.

On Your timing may we depend,
For in doing so our worries will soon suspend.

In Your open arms may we lovingly lean.
May we soothe our souls.
May we have Your peaceful patience to glean!

Lord, when we passionately pursue Your embrace,
That is when all fear can displace!

Punctuated Prayer

Self-Doubt, Faith, and All That is Fantabulous

Have you ever doubted yourself? Perhaps the doubt spiraled from a poignant place like pursuing your heart's passion, or maybe it stemmed from a more mundane goal of simply following through with your daily serving of Green Giant vegetables. Regardless of its form, how did your heart ultimately *shout at the doubt*?

It took quite some time to compose this punctuated prayer, as the foundation of the answer, at least for me, is *faith*. Propelled by sheer curiosity, I sought out the various definitions of faith. I was especially interested in consulting the dictionary's definition of faith. My fingers danced across the keyboard in anticipation of Google's glossary. After briefly smiling at the rainbow hues decorating the search engine's legendary typeface – my digital version of stopping and smelling the roses – I perused the different definitions. The first two Dictionary.com definitions proved particularly interesting because of their versatile appeal. They read: "complete confidence or trust in a person or thing (i.e., faith in another's ability); or a belief not based on proof" (2015).

Ponder the meaning of "complete" for a second, because for many of us, that is often the *mystery* of faith. The ironic part is that the complexity of "complete" can actually be quite simple if we think about what it means to believe in something bigger than ourselves. Much, much bigger! When we live for a grander purpose, when we *humble* ourselves to something beyond human comprehension – something that extends beyond the limited surface area of our cerebral cortices, faith becomes a quite straightforward concept.

From a logical and "let's just get real" standpoint, is it not just *exhausting* trying to control everything? There is only so much we can do without something that we did not plan for swooping in and flipping everything totally upside down! We can passionately prepare only to have the undulating, unruly waves of life rock our boat.

Yet, here is the kicker. *What if* we perceived the "rocking of the boat" as an opportunity to surrender to *all* that is for our greater good? What if we chose to linger in the letting go of it all? What if the seemingly wayward waves rippling from that rocking boat were not actually dangerous currents to be feared, but graceful avenues upon which to carry us to something *better*?

Think back to some of the most seminal moments in your life where you did not achieve something you were initially so adamant to believe was "the perfect thing for you at the perfect time." Then something *unbelievably unplanned* transpired - something of epic proportion that was *much better* than anything your heart or mind could fathom! Remembering those instances helps fortify our faith. It helps us yield to the reality that it is all working together for *fantabulousness* – for the greater good and for gorgeous grace!

It is when we surrender that we ultimately see.

It is when we let go that we can easily place "complete trust or confidence in something," as Dictionary.com denotes. My punctuated prayer for you is to soak in the sweet splendor of faith. Perhaps it involves strengthening that faith on an external level. Or maybe it is an act of fostering further faith in your *truest self and deepest of dreams*. At the end of the day, know that you are doing the best that you can with what you have been given at this very moment. And, remember, everything is going to blossom just as it blissfully should!

Love, Kindness, and Joy

Color The World with Kindness

Lord, teach us to be amazing artists of kindness
In the magnificent masterpiece that is life.

Cultivate an ever-present excitement within our beings
That views spreading kindness as fun,
Always underscoring the vibrant reality that *we are all one*!

My, how You thoughtfully bestowed each and every heart
With a cornucopia of creative gifts!
Who are we *not* to use those shimmering personality shades
For all that is meant to uplift!

We pray that You paint a powerful portrait of compassion in every mind,
For that will awaken our spirits to the sparkly goodness of being kind!

Shine

Lord, may you remind all hearts that they were made to shine!
For they are super duper sparks of all that is Divine!
Secure a peace in their spirits that rings this statement sound and true,
As we are *all* an emanation of You!

Live in Love

Lord, may we understand the following:
To *see* love is to *be* love.
And to *be* love is to *see* love.

May we seek all that is of love in every place,
For this is certain to awaken our spirits to the truest type of love,
The kind that resides within *our own* heart space!

May we regard one another as an emanation of a vastly grander Love.
In doing this, we can then recognize
There is *nothing* to live in fear of!

Love is Air

Lord, may we remember that love is air.
When it is love that we inhale and exhale,
It is kindness and joy that will prevail!

May every breath we utter toward another
Carry a sweet sentiment of encouragement,
As that can be the ultimate spiritual nourishment!

May every hello and goodbye *oxygenate* the day with added love.
For in making each heart feel a little lighter,
We will help someone's spirit happily soar
With the peaceful grace of a Divine dove!

The Language of Kindness

Lord, teach us the language of love!
May we seek to whisper words of endless encouragement,
As such dazzling discourse fuels a happy heart.
Indeed, it is a simply serene form of emotional nourishment!

May we utter words that convey understanding
And satiate every sparkly soul,
For it is the ongoing exchange of empathy that makes each other feel whole!

Lord, inspire speech that softens the spirit and ignites the *ultimate* glow,
Because this is where our shared humanity can bud.
This is where the notion of *one love* can truly grow!

Let the colorful kindness underlying our hello's and goodbye's
Be a heaping and heart-happy serving of spiritual nutrition.
In seeing how unconditional love sparkles like the most majestic sunrise,
We can then understand how such compassion comes to fruition!

Love Triumphs Over Hate

Lord, slow our speech to an empathic, kind, and gentle rate.
May we grow more mindful of how we can speak volumes of loving-kindness
Instead of heart-heaviness and hate.

With those whom we may disagree,
Enlighten our hearts to the beauty of what it means to appreciate,
What it means to blindly accept.
For it is upon this open bed of communication
Where our love for one another can be most adept!

May each sentence emerge from an understanding heart,
And may our language be one of *universal love*.
This is the type of compassion that will bind humankind.
This is Your illuminating illustration with which we can always seek to be aligned.

Divine Diversities

Lord, may we dance to the tune of our dazzling diversities,
For in doing so we can overcome astounding adversities!

May we strum a collective chord of kindness.
May we celebrate all that makes us uniquely neat.
In compassionately composing such a marvelous musical score,
We will be encouraged to live as *one happy heartbeat!*

Harboring Habits of Kindness

Lord, may our habits hug the world with endless forgiveness, love, and kindness.
May our thoughts and behaviors dissolve all fear.
May every mannerism radiate rainbows of niceness!

May the scale of our compassion invite a magnificent curiosity.
The type where others have no choice but to attribute it to the power of prayer
And Your loving luminosity!

May Kindness Bind Us

Lord, help us to sense Your light in each passerby,
Whether stranger or friend,
May we see each other as the same.
May we recognize *You* as our common tie!

You are the inextricable thread that weaves all of us into one;
In the reflection of Your love-light,
There is no need to judge.
There is no need to shun.

Lord, may we regard the strength of Your love
As our ultimate bonding agent,
Linking our lives through compassionate daily engagement!

May we seek to sincerely greet and welcome others.
Just as they are.
Our spiritual sisters and brothers!

May We Be of Service

Lord, inspire us to serve other souls.
For some of the purest pursuits in life center on cultivating kindness goals.

May You carve out a path where we can lighten a stranger's burden.
May our compassionate hearts merge into highways of hope;
For every random gesture of love
Curves into another course for helping someone cope.

While we work to build individual roads of rest,
May we continue to pray for a world that enacts collective kindness.
For such a loving request
Will cause many hearts in need to feel worthy and blessed!

Shatter the Frenzy of Envy

Lord, we reside in an ever-winding world of constant comparison;
A seemingly trying and tiring test
To always win the title of "the best."

Rather than battle for the status of first place,
May our hearts inhabit a more collective space!

Lord, help us to stray from the role of "judge,"
For this will prevent us from harboring any envious grudge.

May we celebrate our neighbors' successes.
May we adopt an attitude
That reflects the love and humility embedded in many Beatitudes!

Encourage us to nurture an immensely *inclusive* and *joyous* love for one another,
The kind where our *shared, happy-hearted humanity*
Can constantly be discovered.

Hope to Hold On
Dedicated to any hearts affected by depression

Lord, may we act as a *fortress* of love for hopeless hearts,
Always seeking to build each other up,
Making one another feel that much stronger.
For *all of the hearts* who have been dwindled by fear and hopelessness,
May we help them hold on a little longer.

Lord, outfit these hearts in an unbreakable armor of faith.
Sturdy their spirits with a newfound hope that shatters all despair.
May they be *lifted* by Your love and *know* that others care.
May their hearts cease to tear.

Lord, inspire us to offer an open ear or a healing hand to hold.
May our words, along with the Holy Spirit, remind these souls
Of every endearing and compassionate complement they have *ever* been told!

Encourage us to sit with them and simply BE,
For such gentle silence can echo lasting love in the most deserted of hearts.
It can be *just what they need* again to feel hope-*full* and free!

Bestowing Joy in a Stranger's Heart

Lord, grace those who we pass today with the utmost joy!
May they feel jubilant in such a way that they exclaim,
"Boy, oh boy!"

Whether it is a fantabulous friend or sparkly stranger,
Bless them with a bold bliss that will deflate any feeling of danger.
Mile after mile, spark their spirits with a sensational smile!

Finding Joy in the Journey

Lord, may we seek joy in the journey.
As we continue to open our hearts to Your will,
May we perceive that calling as the ultimate thrill.

Instead of losing ourselves in useless worry,
Help our hearts bud in the beauty of being still.
Restrain any nagging need to hurry.

Your answers will unfold,
Just as You always told.

In the meantime, may we wondrously welcome life's shifting topography.
With every twist and turn,
May we cultivate an excitement for diving into every detour,
Deeming each "deviation" from our earthly roadmap
As a Divine opportunity to grow and learn!

Joy Please

Lord, swell our hearts with an inexplicable joy!
May You grace us with the kind of happiness that is unparalleled,
In which nothing compares nor feels the same.
May it be an oh-so-sparkly spiritual smile
Where we cannot help but know it derived in Your name!

Surge within our souls a purely happenstance and bursting bliss.
May we praise Your name as we gaze adoringly toward the sky.
For in our heart of hearts, we know that such ecstasy
Pours forth from Your Heavenly supply!

Love Knows No Measure

Lord, thank You immensely for Your gift of unfailing love.
Your compassion is the most invaluable and terrific treasure.
It knows no bounds!
It bears no measure!

What a blessing
To be clothed in a love that is the *ultimate* Divine dressing.

May the unconditional nature of Your love
Inspire our hearts to sprinkle more goodness throughout our daily lives,
Freeing our neighbors from feeling forlorn.
For to nourish our world with amazing acts of altruism
Is to allow a healing haven of humanity to be born!

Punctuated Prayer

The Mathematics of Love

    Math was never my forte. While I may veer from all that is Sine, Cosine, and Tangent, I always appreciated the power in numbers. From the moment I created Lunchtime Love – an organization that serves Chicagoans in need by decorating and distributing meals with messages of love, hope, faith, and encouragement – the impact of collective acts of love and kindness blossomed in a whole new light.

    The inaugural Lunchtime Love event occurred in July of 2015, in Chicago's Millennium Park. I practically skipped onto the patch of grass that would soon be the home of future Lunchtime Love gatherings. Outfitted in heart-shaped sunglasses, a crimson red top, and lovingly loud leopard-print leggings, I was in my "love and kindness" element. The sunshiny smile stretched across my face spoke volumes; I could not contain the glee as I waited for others to join in on the goodness. I giddily arranged twenty pre-packed lunch bags into a heart shape throughout the lush green grass. I took a moment to pause and ponder God's grace. I needed to soak it all in. Other than my fantabulous friend, Taylor, I had no idea what to expect in terms of the total number of attendees. Nor could I fathom the radiant responses of passersby ambling along Michigan Avenue, which was adjacent to the Lunchtime Love location. I had no inkling of the sweetly stirring stories I would be privileged to hear. I could not forecast the beautiful new hearts I would meet on that sparkling summer afternoon. Despite encountering more than a few mishaps in the event planning process, I did not feel nervous. Instead, my spirit felt as if it were cloaked with a blanket of palpable peace! The stillness of my soul served as a whisper of God's all-loving and all-encompassing presence. Whatever transpired that afternoon would stem from complete compassion! *Love* was all I needed to know.

    I wholeheartedly believe in the infinite influence of love. Moreover, when kindness is cooperative, its impact attests to the *exponential* power of love. There is a miraculous magnetism in performing random acts of kindness; the more hearts we seek to heal on a daily basis, the more we experience the fantastic force field of love throughout our world!

    Not long after I concluded setting up for the event, my gaze centered on one of the most sincere smiles I had ever seen. It belonged to my new friend, Tate, who radiated that kind of genuine spirit and pure loving heart that reminds you why this world is such a beautiful place. His optimism was infectious! He peppered our conversation with rhymes about butterflies and bees. He harnessed an innate gift for the type of poetry that punctuates the heart with positivity. Yet, Tate's astounding penchant for spreading love and kindness extended beyond his encouraging "notes of hope." When my friend, Julia, shared the recent challenges of navigating her new city of Chicago, Tate joyfully jumped at the opportunity to make her feel at home. He insisted on leaving his lunch and dashed across Michigan Avenue to the Chicago Cultural Center. As he ran across the bustling street, our jaws dropped in astonishment. Our hearts were in awe of Tate's immediate kindness. He ultimately returned with a paper map of Chicago's city streets and landmarks. Something tells me Tate's heart exudes such kindness on a daily basis, not to mention he thrives on any opportunity to make others feel more at ease, more loved! He is surely an angelic soul, and the world is undoubtedly a brighter place because of his effervescent personality.

    Tate's empathy for Julia's journey was just one of the countless acts of lunchtime love we observed that day. The entire day was a miracle magnifying the mathematics of love. All in all, there were only four of us who actually composed "notes of hope" for homeless Chicagoans. A total of twenty lunches were distributed. Yet, therein lies the healing power of several hearts working together for the greater good of our humanity. Who *knows* how many fellow passersby continued the kindness ripple that day, simply by observing love in motion!

    My prayer for you is to go out and be a love mathematician! One person *can* make miracles of difference. It only takes one act of genuine compassion to multiply love on a level that impacts millions of hearts. Because *love* is our common denominator, the equation for spreading goodness and joy in this world is quite simple. My prayer is that we strive to live *with*, *in*, and *for* love in every moment of every day. For this is a formula bound to help love make a way!

Gratitude and Mindfulness

Gratitude

Lord, inspire a glorious gratitude
In every mindful motion.
For the thrill of thankfulness is bound to calm every inner commotion.

Thank You for Being You

Lord, grace our whole beings with gratitude,
For it is the most exhilarating attitude!
May we envision
All that we encounter as if it were wrapped in a radiant ribbon!

May we deem our successes and failures as a never-ending gift,
Because it is in giving thorough thanks for *all* we experience
That grants every soul the ultimate lift!

From eyesight
To scent
To taste
To hearing
To touch.
My, how You blessed us with so much!

Lord, thank You for being you!

The Majestic

Lord, may we marvel at the majestic!
Losing ourselves in the boundless beauty You created
Surely erases all that is hectic.

Make our hearts proud
At the sight of every captivating cloud!
May the serenely sparkling sun
Remind us that through You,
It has all been done!

The cerulean sky!
My! Oh! My!
Lord, thank You for the glory
That shines throughout nature's story!

To Listen Is to Glisten

Lord, may we regard nature as an earthly "BLESSON:"
Both a love lesson and beautiful blessing.
My, Lord, how Your Divine creation is all-caressing!

May we be invigorated by the spunky scamper of a passing squirrel.
With each faith-*full* footstep,
May our sense of awe inspire us to joyfully jump and twirl!

For You are present in every blissful breeze that kisses our cheeks.
You *are* the serendipitous sparkle shimmering down every stream.
Lord, may our jaws drop in amazement at how Your glory gleams!

Within the whistling weather may we wonder at Your word.
May we listen as *You* glisten!

May every step unlock a newfound appreciation for a crispy, colorful fall leaf.
For the stillness of the present moment is a restorative rock for our spirits;
The ultimate relief!

Lord, You exist in us
And we exist in You.
It surely is a BLESSON to have nature help us recognize
That this is terrifically true!

Nature's Cure

Lord, may we never cease to marvel at nature's boundless beauty and grace.
For it is a radiant reminder that You are present in every serene space.

You surely furnished every forest with the most fantabulous foliage!
From babbling brooks to dazzling deer,
Your magnificence truly envelops us.
You *are* always near!

May the wind sing a song that stills our souls.
For such miracles are further affirmation
That nature is a majestic and mindful means to console!

Embracing the Wonder of a New Week

Lord, may our hearts ooze in AWE-some appreciation for the new week!
May Monday be marvelous and miraculous.
May it be a mindful means to experience You in all which we seek.

What a miracle it is to embrace something anew,
For that is yet another glorious gateway to include You in all that we do!

May we dance in the divinity of every new opportunity.
May we interject our day with random acts of kindness that fortify our community!

Lord, radiantly remind us to chase an attitude of gratitude.
And when all appears to be a cloudy craze,
Feel free to chime in and amaze!

Morning Miracles

Lord, may we be amazed by the radiant rays!
May we be mindful of every miracle,
And the incomparable beauty of nature's ways.

May we perceive the tie-dye sky
As a landscape of endless love.
A *true miracle* from the Most High.

May every cushiony cloud
Make our hearts peaceful and proud!

Lord, what a *blessing* it is to be alive!
Remind us to seek the magic in every morning sunrise,
May our souls soak in each ray of sunshine
As if we were peering through a new pair of eyes
For the very first time!

Serenity of a Sunset

Lord, may we gasp in gratitude for the happy hues dancing across the evening skies.
My, how You painted a gorgeous grandeur with the most peaceful palette!
May every stunning sunset always render us speechless,
And unload the most serene of sighs!

Aaaaahhhh!

From baby blue to outstanding orange to cheerful yellow,
My, how every color induces *all* that feels mellow!
As the sun subtly yet powerfully dips its radiant rays below the healing horizon,
May that glorious and graceful glow
Be the ultimate blessing to feast our eyes on!

Punctuated Prayer

Laundry and Gratitude

What does laundry have to do with gratitude? Put simply, it has loads to do with it! As a little girl, I vividly recall burying my face into the heaping pile of freshly washed, hot-out-of-the-dryer towels. It did not matter whether our Chicago forecast predicted a temperature of 10 or 100 degrees. There was something magical about the stark sensation of warm towels against my skin – I could not help but melt into the moment! I could not focus on anything else because every inch of me was yearning to prolong those cozy feelings. I was like the child-size version of Snuggle the Bear; cuddling with those towels induced an unparalleled cheerfulness. Although at 6-years-old I may not have directly linked laundry-time love with an appreciation for life's little blessings, now I cannot help but draw the parallel.

It was no coincidence that this exercise in gratitude occurred the day prior to one of my Lunchtime Love events. In the midst of preparation, I decided to do a last-minute load of laundry. After I removed the clothes from the dryer, I draped them across my bed with the intent to fold them later. However, something delightfully deterred me from doing just that. Perhaps it was the fact that I craved a mini-mindfulness break. Or, maybe it was the wonderful warmth of just-dried clothing radiating across my skin, causing a gazillion goose bumps to skip across my arms. Regardless, I was instantly transported back to those laundry-time love moments of my childhood. I remembered gleefully diving into that mountain of toasty towels, covered in joy! This time, however, I understood such joy as an avenue to cultivating gratitude.

An amazing awareness and appreciation for the seemingly little, yet not-so-little things of life flooded my heart. I thanked God profusely for the privilege of the ability to do laundry in my own apartment. I thanked God for *having* clothes to wash. I thanked God for the *option* to do laundry while completing other activities on my to-do list. Multi-tasking never proved more miraculous!

There are countless individuals in need who would consider such routine "chores" as the greatest grace granted by God. Likewise, it is no small blessing to have the physical *mobility* to transfer laundry from the washer/dryer to my bed, much less to have a mattress to sleep on!

Thus, my prayer for you is twofold: to recognize the innate power of *experiencing* gratitude, and to inspire your heart to unearth the blessing in every "to-do" of your daily routine. Regarding the former, may you remember that to merely *feel* gratitude is a gift – it is grace! Not only does gratitude open our hearts to life's blessings, but it also encourages us to cherish every single moment on this earth. If we peacefully ponder the sheer joy granted through the practice of gratitude, its gift will be unveiled. *Every opportunity* to express thankfulness is its own grace! Gratitude is like a sweet cake of boundless blessings; layer after lovingly layer, there resides a deliciously sweet blessing for our souls to feast on!

I pray that this inspires you to increasingly see the trivial as a terrific treasure! When we strive to count our blessings – big and small – we can then bask in the joy of it all!

The Power of Prayer

Pervasive Prayer

Lord, tune our hearts with a love song that echoes the power of prayer.
Whether we pray standing up, driving in the car, on a walk, or bent on one knee,
May we always remember that Your word will set us free.
And on many occasions, even make us want to joyfully shout out in glee!

Help us to constantly seek Your will above our own,
Remind us to reflect on the array of answers granted to previous prayers,
As Your supremely loving wisdom and grander purpose has always been shown!

May prayer fit us like the coziest spiritual clothing;
AWE-some attire that we cannot wait to wear!
Lord, to know that You are just a prayer away
Is to know that you are *all there*.
You are everywhere.

Effortless Prayer

Lord, invite us to pray in a faithfully fresh and novel way!

May You act as author and may our hearts be Your pen,
For when our prayers our aligned with Your word and will,
That is our true zen!

As our souls heed Your inspiration,
May we breathe in and out
All that calms every debilitating doubt.

Often we pray for only what the earthly eye can see.
But Lord, from Your Heavenly position,
You will always know what we truly need!

Harken our hearts to write a prayer
That underlines the virtues of Your divine book.
Gosh knows, as we re-read the story of our lives,
Many times a prayer of trust was all it took!

Praying for a Stranger

Lord, teach us how to pray for another despite not knowing the need or desire.
Perhaps the prayer can simply suffice as one of strength.
A heart song that helps a stranger surmount the day's challenges.
An intention that aims to instill peace of heart with however the day transpires.

We may not have the perfect phrase or right word.
But may we at least pray for all strangers,
And for *their* prayers to be happily heard.

As always, may we be mindful of the worthiness of every prayer,
In every heart.
For *this* is the most faithful start.

Sharing the Power of Prayer

Lord, we joyously thank You for every opportunity to share
The power of prayer!

May our daily dialogue with a stranger or friend
Underscore that in *Your* own way,
To *every* prayer,
You *always* tend.

Whether or not we unveiled the nature or timing of a personal prayer to another,
May these AMAZE-ing conversations remind us
That You hear every prayer loud and clear.
Lord, may the smiles sewn across our stories
Grant complete confidence that You are always near.
In Your merciful might and the communion of prayer,
We truly have nothing to fear!

In contemplating the "when", "where", "why," and "how" of every prayer,
May many of our daily exchanges reveal
How often Your answers emerge in another's story.
My, how this is a fantabulous reflection of Your loving glory!

Not only will this attest to a transformative truth,
Namely that prayer soothes the soul.
But also it will make everything feel all right.
We will be elated at how the power of prayer can *unite*!

May We See the Divine in Every Sign

Lord, may we search for Your will in every sign.
For when we are enlightened with the truth that You reside in all things,
That is precisely when our authenticity sings.
That is when we can feel our wonderful wings!

May we surrender our plans to Your wise ways,
All the while offering You the utmost thanks and praise.

When we pray for a path to be paved,
Teach us to forgo words like "me" and "mine."
For that only obscures all the gifts which emanate from the Divine.

May we pray in a voice that underscores why *You* make the ultimate choice.
When it comes to discerning Your will,
Steer our hearts toward words like "Yours,"
As that is when You reveal our deepest destinies.
Lord, that is when *You* open the doors!

Forgiveness and Healing

Forgiveness

Lord, what is it to *truly* forgive?
Why, it is to truly *live*!

When we release resentment,
We open our spirits to a newfound contentment.

Help us surrender eons of anger,
For they only grip us like a stiff, constricting hanger.

Let us linger in the "letting go,"
Because to fully love another and ourselves,
Without limitations,
That is when we can be privy to *know*.

To know what it means to feel lightness of spirit.
Oh Lord, help us hear it!

May Your endless example of loving-kindness
Endeavor us to embrace joy yet again.
May we un-tether our spirits in a way
That channels non-judgment and abundant acceptance.
For that is the point where peace of mind can find its entrance.

That is when we can fully release.
That is when we can instantly allow our souls to prance in a palpable peace!

Release the Affliction of Addiction

Lord, heal hearts from the affliction of addiction.
Although it suffocates the soul
And induces an incessant feeling of emptiness and need,
Just a touch of Your grace and mercy can swiftly supersede!

Take away their pulsating pain
By filling that deeply voracious void with Your glorious gain.
For *all* can be healed in Thy name!

With Your serenity, love, and kindness,
You will always save.
Because, in the end, it is Your infinite loving comfort they truly crave!

Traversing the Tragedy

Lord, may You grant us a profound peace to cope with traumas and tragedies,
As their onsets remain as some of life's most daunting mysteries.

Whether they manifest as acts of war against our fellow neighbors,
Or sicknesses one does not deserve,
Please grace us with an endless comfort
With which our hearts can always preserve.

When these events transpire,
Our spirits cannot help but tire.
Their enigmatic nature seem to twist our minds into a maze,
Inciting a hectic haze.

However, the truth is that much of life is out of our control.
Lord, may Your grace and mercy lessen that spiritual toll.

Remind us that it is normal and healthy to experience grief.
Yet, we ask that You hug our hearts along the way,
As this will undoubtedly provide the mending we need!

In shining down Your healing light,
May we recognize that as arduous as it may be to *fully* feel,
To do so is surely a means to *heal*.

Grant us the patience to wait for Your answers.
Even though we may never understand Your ways,
One thing is true.
When we observe all that is good and loving in this world,
We can know such serenity stems from You.

Let the Light In

Lord, some days are harder than others.
Our hearts bear the weight of impatience and fear.
For this reason, may the peace of prayer permeate all aspects of life,
May we lean on You fully and faithfully,
As this is sure to rid of any suffocating internal strife.

Lord, restore a bountiful breath.
Lift the fright by shining down a lasting love,
The kind that is beyond brilliantly bright!
By sheer grace, may we veer towards all that is valiant.
May our prayers for more ardent faith help us stand upright!

Now, more than ever,
We need to feel Your light.
We *yearn* to be strengthened by Your merciful and ever-miraculous might!

Lord, when our souls feel drained and dark,
Be our spiritual spark!
May we imagine many a rainbow and its hope-*full* arc!

Flood our hearts with a love-light that penetrates every cell.
For when You take the radiant reigns,
When *You* dissolve the pain,
We know that all will be well.

And for those experiences that serve as some of our truest spiritual teachers,
Surround us with extra angels
So that we may endure.
So that we may feel lovingly secure!

Still the Stresses

Lord, whether it is an inundation of myriad mini stressors,
Or a larger battle,
Cloak our spirits with a blanket of stillness and strength.
May Your mercy be palpable.
May it calm any internal rattle.

As elusive as the answers seem to be,
May we cull from the Holy Spirit, angels, and saints
Lightness of heart and waves of serenity!

Punctuated Prayer
Addiction, Acceptance, and the Power of Unconditional Love

How many times have you heard the old adage, "Don't judge a book by its cover?" What sentiments and memories stir within your heart as you reflect on these words? How many involved personal interactions or encounters where you walked away only to delightfully discover that your initial perception was slightly clouded – or, in some cases, overwhelmingly overcast?

We reside in a world where our net self-worth is often measured by material possessions, social status, and the number of "likes" garnered from the most recent social media post. Yet, if we ponder these social measuring sticks, we recognize that their contents are transient. The surge of instant gratification is anything but enduring for our human hearts.

So, then, *what truly lasts in this life?*

Love. Love lasts.

The love we harbor for family and friends remains one of life's grandest treasures. Yet, what if that love elevated to a level that encompassed strangers? I believe we are born with the innate ability to love *anyone* unconditionally, for the very simple reason that *we are all connected*. Moreover, nurturing such an enduring love emerges from practicing empathy, forgiveness, and endless compassion. Such graces are paramount for loving the seemingly un-loveable – the individuals with the most worn "book covers." Unconditional love finds some of its most restorative power when expressed toward those who have lost their way. Whether the detour resulted from uncontrollable circumstances or unfortunate decision-making, it does not detract from the fact that every heart is worthy of true love and mercy.

One of the most blessed ways in which I have experienced the healing energy of unconditional love and acceptance stemmed from my relationships with individuals in need. Without a doubt, those friends who have little to nothing are some of the most resilient, faithful, and gentle souls I have ever encountered. It is difficult to elucidate why my heart has always been pulled to befriending individuals within the homeless community. While I attribute a significant part of it to spiritual reasons, it also stems from my experience in overcoming a years-long addiction. The circumstances surrounding my addiction and recovery do not remotely compare to the trials suffered on the streets. For one, the label, homeless, is inherently weighed down by a debilitating societal stigma. While I can never pretend to understand such a struggle, I empathize with the suffocating feelings of judgment and isolation. I understand the crippling feelings of self-doubt and confusion that arise when faith is tested to its core. Nevertheless, I do not regret that chapter of my life because it opened my soul to a narrative of empathy. It ignited my spirit with a light that continues to illuminate the value of accepting every heart for *all* of who they are – no questions asked. No heart is immune from experiencing trials and tribulations, as that is embedded in the human experience. Yet, *imagine* the cooperative resiliency that would bloom if we helped each other traverse those trials *together*. To recognize that we are not alone in our challenges is beyond transformative!

To fully appreciate the healing power of unconditional love and empathy, we must imagine what it feels like to be homeless. Imagine not knowing the origins of your next meal. Imagine dedicating most of your energy to determining which locations will provide the most refuge from theft or abuse. Imagine sitting on a flimsy plastic crate in the midst of a bustling city, during winter temperatures that have a negative wind chill advisory. Imagine worrying about whether you will receive just enough change to cover the necessary fare so that you can sleep on a heated train through all hours of the night. Imagine doing all of this while praying to catch the gaze of a passerby – *praying to feel like you matter*.

Now, imagine what it would feel like to see the sparkle of a smile directed toward your face! Imagine what it would feel like to hear a simple "hello." Imagine how a stranger's genuine interest in the course of your day could peacefully pierce what was once the saddest silence in your soul. Imagine your heart swelling with the joy of feeling loved and accepted simply because you are you!

So, how does such an exercise in empathy relate to book covers? It is through empathizing with another's plight that we come to learn the full story. To empathize is for our hearts to surrender to a stranger's story, walking heart-in-heart as they turn the pages to the hope of a new day. To empathize is *to listen with love*. When we listen without judgment, we help other souls piece together the pages of their unique life novels. Ultimately, we are all covered in worn dust jackets. Why not work together to author a new chapter of unconditional love and compassion! In time, such compassion can craft a new story – one that opens our souls to the following plot: it is what is on the inside that truly matters.

My prayer for you is to dedicate more of your daily heart space to loving unconditionally. Take a moment to celebrate someone in need just because you can – because you *want* to. Listen, converse, or simply just BE with them in that moment. May your kindness echo the precious treasure that is another's heart! And, always remember, every act of compassion combines to form a connective tissue of unconditional love around our entire world!

Authenticity

Authentic Self

Lord, help us discover the delight of living life as our truest selves,
As doing so propels us to a place where we can fully thrive.
It opens our hearts to the experience
Of what it means to feel amazingly alive!

May we champion every quirk.
For You created us with a marvelous uniqueness
That we should never shirk.

Restrain our hearts from worrying about what others think.
Release any constricting chains of self-doubt.
Instead, redistribute our energy to all that is dazzlingly devout.

Lord, when we mold our thoughts and actions around You,
That is when our hearts can recline.
That is when our souls can dive into the peace of the Divine!

To cherish all that makes us unique
Is to realize what it feels like for our *entire* spirits to truly speak!

Genuine

Lord, may we invest in our individuality
And witness the wonderful in all that is weird.
For our unique facets serve as something to be revered!

Help us to catch our inner critic,
And replace it with *total* self-love.
For to be created in Your image is a blessing to be in awe of!

May we not fear painting the world with our vivid heart hues.
Because when we entirely embrace *all* of whom we are,
We honor You,
And we surely have nothing to lose!

Lord, help us remember that contrast
Often serves as the allure of astounding art.
In this way, we can better recognize how our peculiar patterns and asymmetry
Work to enact an inimitable purpose for *every* personality part!

Punctuated Prayer

Be Your Best Self by Immersing Yourself in Imperfection

An exceptionally wise friend of mine, Cassius, once relayed one of his favorite quotes by Abraham Lincoln: "No matter what you are, be your best." These words reverberated in my heart space for a few days. President Lincoln's message encompasses much more than the physical and emotional exertion underlying our "best" endeavors. His message also speaks to the beauty of *imperfection, non-judgment,* and *gentleness of spirit.*

Gentleness may seem ironic given that "best" often connotes images of our hearts "leaving it all on the field" or emulating all that is Rocky Balboa. While I wholeheartedly champion this type of energy in pursuing one's personal best, there is something to be said for practicing gentleness of spirit. Gentleness, in the context of "being your best," entails a retraction from self-judgment - *a detour from chasing perfectionism.* I believe it is pivotal to touch upon the latter, as there is an unparalleled grace in *celebrating* all that is imperfect in this life. To be downright honest, I certainly have days where I need to tap the mindfulness well for more awareness of the following reality: *there is no such thing as perfect!* In an effort to let this mindfully digest deep within our sparkly souls, simply channel your inner Dorothy from The Wizard of Oz (clicking your heels is optional):

> There is no such thing as perfect.
> There is no such thing as perfect.
> There is no such thing as perfect.
> You *are* human!

By *immersing ourselves in the imperfect,* we plant seeds of self-love. And, this self-love allows our hearts to beat with greater empathy for our world. How can we "be our best" if we do not welcome mistakes and failures as propellers for self-growth – for love-learning?

In a culture where perfectionism is praised, why not give our strained spirits a breather? In a world where the imperfect seeks to be invisible, why not blaze a nifty new trail? Instead of depleting our spirit of self-worth and inner-sparkle, perhaps we dare to be our best at *mastering imperfection.* In this way, we can learn to honor our truest, most authentic selves! Maybe we grow gentler in the development of our goal-driven thought processes. While aiming for awesomeness, let us not penalize our hearts for missing the mark.

On the same token, how beautiful would it be if we *celebrated* our neighbors' successes! What if we *lived in radical love for each other*? What if we *collectively corroded* any comparison tendencies? By serving as each other's cheerleaders, we can start to envision "the best" through a lens of compassionate collaboration! By encouraging another person to be his or her best, we can invigorate our utmost potential. Even more, *we can be our best at being ourselves* – our fullest, most YOU-nique selves.

My prayer for you is to embark on a journey of tenderness. Delight in the direction of self-love as it blossoms from all that is imperfect. It could be as easy as laughing at yourself when you make a mistake or humbling yourself by asking for help when you need it most. Perhaps the simplest route is recognizing that you are already a winner just by being yourself! And, that only means that everything you need to "be your best" already resides *within* you!

Dreams

Dazzling Dreams

Lord, when we dream, may we strive to lovingly listen.
For to do so fully and faithfully,
Our hearts cannot help but glisten!

May we dream vividly.
May we dream in color.
And may we delightfully dream for *total goodness* to grace one another!

Miracles manifest in myriad ways, each and every day!
What our sparkly spirits can *conceive*,
May we know that with unrelenting hope, deep determination, and fervent faith,
You will help us radiantly receive!

Wisdom, Patience, and Understanding

Divine Decisions

Lord, You reign as our spiritual sage.
Within our earthly books,
You can anticipate every word,
Every page.

May You instill in us a sacred approach to decision-making,
For to garner Your guidance *first and foremost*
Is sure to keep our conscience from shaking.

Whether the resolution we seek is rooted in something big or small,
We know that heeding Your providence
Will help us make the most prudent call.

In navigating our decision-making route,
May You lead us to spiritual signs that help eradicate self-doubt.

Enhance our awareness of any feelings
That align with profound inner peace and calm.
For often these are signs sparked by the Holy Spirit.
They are a Heavenly cue
That the answers we desire are in clear view,
Opening our hearts to experience something Divinely anew!

Teamwork

Lord, as our minds incessantly calculate the course of the day's events,
Help us refrain from controlling every detail on our own.
Instead, may we request Your presence in *every* moment,
Always taking refuge in the fact that we do not have to embark on our journeys alone.

May we remember that our guardian angels are joyously waiting for us
To invite their guidance and protection.
They are eager to help us do our best
While avoiding the pitfalls of pursuing perfection.

Lord, may we envision the day's responsibilities as a team.
To do so will fortify our faith.
It will remind us that at any point,
We can pray for Your *peace* to intervene.

Fear Cannot Take Pride Where Love Resides

Lord, when living in accordance with Your will,
May we be confident that we are doing Your Divine work.
May we experience a tranquility of soul,
Where discouragement and self-doubt have nowhere to lurk.
Instead, we feel wonderfully whole!

With You, there is no challenge too small or too great.
When our efforts find an ally in *Your* love,
Fear will always be too late!

Walking in the Waiting

Lord, grant us Your wondrous wisdom to wait.
Hold our hands and teach us to walk with a peace-*full*, patient gait.

Your spiritual blueprints were etched out so thoughtfully,
Gracefully guiding our earthly lives.
Why, then, should unnecessary worry induce inner strife?
If You truly know what is best,
Why do we continue to test?

We pray to do our best,
But may You regularly remind us that only *You* know the rest!

Rising Above

Lord, may we seek to grow leaps and bounds
As we approach our daily rounds!
Fashion our spirits with a resilience that we have never before seen!
All throughout the day,
In every miraculous moment,
May we find You in the space between!

Harvest within our hearts spiritual fruits such as gentleness and joy.
Perhaps much, much more!
May we welcome any suffering as a means for spurring strength.
May it prepare us for *all* that You have in store!

And, Lord, if we tire,
May we rest in hope and the Holy Spirit.
For it is during these times when You often *most* inspire!

Humility

Humble Hearts

Lord, teach us how to be marvelously meek.
Harbor within our hearts hope to be happily humble.
Modesty helps us evade pride,
Which is bound to make us tumble.

Within our heart space please plant serene seeds of endless empathy.
For when we walk in humility,
That is when we understand our shared humanity.

Humble Dreams

Lord, may we dream big while remaining humble.
As grand as our visions may grow,
Maintaining meekness of spirit will help us to not stumble.

May we remember that Your will ascends above our own.
Knowing this helps us surrender to a serene spiritual zone.
Whatever delightful dreams our hearts desire,
May we remain unassuming.
For such humble hope transforms into its own miracle magnifier!

Angels and Miracles

Upon an Angel's Wings

Lord, for every sparkly soul,
May You provide an angel at every angle.
May we feel cozy comfort under many an angel's wing.
May we seek solace in every harmonious song our angels sing.

May we feel at ease surrounded by their loving lightness.
For our angels compassionately carry the heaviest of hearts
To the most Heavenly haven of brightness!

Preparing Miracles for Hearts in Need
A Prayer to Guide Service Work

Lord, may Your presence prevail
As we prepare to feed hope to hearts in need.
May You shine down a shimmering glow.
May Your brilliant love-light glitter all around us
So that everyone will know!

Let the joyous gratitude of giving gleam across our faces.
May such luminosity embody an extension of Your grandest graces.

May we commune in happiness and laughter,
As YOU are the ever-illuminating road to happily ever after!

May every smile, hug, and handshake
Relieve any heavy-hearted memories of past heartbreak.

May our words and behaviors convey the universal message:
"You matter!"
Such seemingly small acts of kindness serve as a vibrant vessel
For a widespread feeling of hope to scatter!

Bless the food and land
Upon which we lend a helping hand.

Lord, may Your miracles astound;
Forever reminding every heart in need
That Your grace and mercy are omnipresent.
Your unconditional love is all around!

Miracle Weather

Lord, may we seek a shower of miracles
And Heavenly surprises today.
For the graceful goodness that drizzles down from above
Is the best forecast for which we can pray!

May we leave *everything* in Your hands,
For Yours are the most marvelous and powerful of plans!

Gratitude for Our Guardian Angels

Lord, may we express thanks for the Heavenly presence of our guardian angels!
In an effort to exude our gratitude,
May we assign each a name in time of serene solitude.

Perhaps we experience their gorgeous glow
As Heavenly phosphorescence.
Maybe it manifests as a more subtle presence.
However we perceive our winged companions,
What a blessing it is to be enveloped by their endearing essence!

Whether wide awake or fast asleep,
Our angels' ongoing protection is the ultimate comfort for our hearts to keep!

Lord, remind us that guidance from our mystical messengers
Is just a prayer away.
As this is bound to transport tranquility into each and every day!

Made in the USA
San Bernardino, CA
15 May 2017